I Didn't Do It!

Written by Sue Graves

Illustrated by
Desideria Guicciardini

W
FRANKLIN WATTS
LONDON•SYDNEY

Poppy didn't always tell the truth at home.

"I didn't do it!" said Poppy.

Sometimes Poppy didn't tell the truth at school either. On Monday, she broke a window during morning playtime.

"I didn't do it!" said Poppy.
She said that **Joe** broke the window.

Miss Plum was cross with Joe. She said he had to stay in for the rest of playtime.

Joe was cross that Poppy didn't **tell the** truth.

Then Poppy spilled water over Meg's painting. Meg was upset.

Poppy said that **Lucy had done it.** Lucy was cross that Poppy didn't tell the truth.

Later on, Lucy forgot to turn off the tap in the cloakroom. Water splashed all over the floor.

Lucy said **Poppy** had done it.

Miss Plum said Poppy was very careless.

13

Poppy was **cross** that Lucy didn't tell the truth.

"Now you know how **we** feel when **you** tell a fib!" said Lucy.

Everyone was cross with Poppy for not telling the truth. At lunchtime, nobody wanted to play with her.
Poppy felt sad.

Poppy **felt bad** for not telling the truth. She went to see Miss Plum. She told her what she had done.

Miss Plum said everyone does something wrong sometimes. She said it was always **better to own up than to tell a fib.**

Miss Plum said that Poppy had to put things right. Poppy nodded.

She felt **sorry for fibbing** and making her friends cross. Poppy told everyone, **"I'm sorry."**

Then Poppy helped Mr Brown mend the broken window. Mr Brown was pleased.

She helped Meg to paint a new picture. Miss Plum put it up on the wall. Meg was pleased.

Then Poppy and Lucy promised Miss Plum to tidy the cloakroom for a **whole week!**

Soon it was afternoon playtime.
Everyone went outside to play.

And this time everyone wanted to play with Poppy!

Can you tell the story of what happens when Ellie doesn't tell the truth?

How do you think Ellie's sister felt when Mum thought she kicked over the pot? Should Ellie tell the truth? Why?

A note about sharing this book

The *Our Emotions and Behaviour* series has been developed to provide a starting point for further discussion on children's feelings and behaviour, both in relation to themselves and to other people.

I Didn't Do It!
This story explores, in a reassuring way, why it is important to tell the truth and the consequences that can follow when the truth is not told.

The book aims to encourage children to have a developing awareness of behavioural expectations in different settings. It also invites children to begin to consider the consequences of their words and actions for themselves and others.

Storyboard puzzle
The wordless storyboard on pages 26 and 27 provides an opportunity for speaking and listening. Children are encouraged to tell the story illustrated in the panels: Ellie doesn't own up to Mum when she knocks over the flower pot, and instead accuses her younger sister. Her sister is angry and hurt and doesn't want to play with Ellie anymore. Ellie realises she has done wrong and apologises to Mum and to her sister. She then puts things right by re-potting the plant. Her little sister is keen to play with her again. Ellie learns that it is better to tell the truth after all.

How to use the book
The book is designed for adults to share with either an individual child, or a group of children, and as a starting point for discussion.

The book also provides visual support and repeated words and phrases to build confidence in children who are starting to read on their own.

Before reading the story
Choose a time to read when you and the children are relaxed and have time to share the story.

Spend time looking at the illustrations and talk about what the book may be about before reading it together.

After reading, talk about the book with the children:

- What was the story about? Have the children not told the truth on occasion? What happened? How did they feel? Did they eventually put things right, and if so, how?

- Have the children ever been wrongly accused of something? What happened? How did they feel?
  Encourage the children to talk about their experiences.

- Talk about the importance of telling the truth. Acknowledge that sometimes it feels like it's hard to tell the truth, but point out that telling a lie often makes things harder later on. Also take the opportunity to point out that it is equally important for adults to tell the truth as it is for children.

- Ask the children why it is important to own up and to apologise if they do something wrong.

- Look at the end of the story again. Poppy felt much better when she started to put things right. Why do the children think this made her feel happier?

- Look at the storyboard puzzle. Ask the children to tell the story in their own words. Why do they think Ellie didn't tell the truth right away? Why was Ellie's sister cross with her and why didn't she want to play with her?

Can the children think of specific times when it is very/especially important to tell the truth?

Choose children to take the parts of Poppy, Miss Plum, Joe, Lucy, Meg and Mr Brown.

Invite them to mime the story as you read the text aloud.

This edition 2015

First published in 2013 by
Franklin Watts
338 Euston Road
London
NW1 3BH

Franklin Watts Australia
Level 17/207 Kent Street
Sydney
NSW 2000

Text © Franklin Watts 2013
Illustrations © Desideria Guicciardini 2013

A CIP catalogue record for this book is available
from the British Library.

ISBN 978 1 4451 3897 8

Editor: Jackie Hamley
Designer: Peter Scoulding

Printed in China

Franklin Watts is a division of
Hachette Children's Books,
an Hachette UK company.
www.hachette.co.uk

FSC
www.fsc.org

MIX
Paper from
responsible sources
FSC® C104740